What Makes a Bird a Bird?

A Bucky and Bingo Learning Adventure

Andi Cann

I hope you enjoy learning about birds today! Please visit my website https://www.andicann.com and register your email address. You will receive a free book and be the first to know about new books, special offers, and free stuff!

If you have a chance, please write a review. It helps other readers and me, an independent author. Thank you!

Andi

Children love nature. Animals are favorites. Birds are especially loved. There are

10,000 types of birds. So, how does one explain the difference between an ostrich

(bird) and a bat (mammal)? What exactly makes a bird a bird? Join Bucky and Bingo

as they learn about the concept of "animal class." Like mammals and reptiles, birds are

members of the Chordata class (made up of vertebrates.) Their scientific name is Aves.

Birds' primary (and only) differentiator is that they have feathers. There are other

organisms that lay eggs, fly, are warm-blooded, have two feet, and possess beaks.

Have fun exploring science with your children!

For my parents who have always supported my love
of reading and birds!

Hi! My name is Bucky and this is my dog, Bingo. He and I love learning together. Today, we are trying to figure out what

makes a bird a bird! Do you want to find out, too?

We found a secret book that tells us about nature and animals. Today, it told us about animals.

A bird is an animal.

A snail is an animal.
Bingo, my dog, is an animal.

Your goldfish and hamster are animals.

All of these animals are different. But some of them are alike.

Bingo and this cow both have fur.

Animals are grouped. Birds are a group. Reptiles are a group. Mammals are a group. Fish, insects, and even dinosaurs are a group (even though they don't exist anymore!)

What makes up a group? What makes a bird a bird? What makes a reptile a reptile? What makes a bug a bug?

What do
you
think?

Let's
think
about it.

What makes birds unique or
special? What is different
about them from your dog?

Birds...lay eggs! Your dog doesn't lay eggs. But birds do. They lay big eggs. Little eggs. Even, red, white, and blue eggs.

But fish, and reptiles, and bugs also lay eggs, so

that's not what makes a bird a bird.

Birds fly! Is that what makes them special? Is that why they are grouped together?

Oh no! Bats, monkeys and, even squirrels fly. And, this ostrich is a bird and it cannot fly.

Hmmm…..that's not it, either.

Birds have two feet. Is that what makes them birds?

Noooo! That's just silly! You and I have two feet and we're not birds!

What about singing and making noise?

There are

birds who "Who" and others who Cock-a-doodle-doo doo.

There are some who trill and others who are shrill. Does singing make a bird a bird?

Nope. Other animals make sounds, too.

What about beaks?   Is THAT
what makes a bird a bird?

Close...but still that's not it. Because this turtle has a beak!

A bird is a bird because it has...FEATHERS! That's right.

A bird is a bird because it has feathers.

It doesn't matter whether it lays eggs or has legs, whether it has a beak or can speak. A bird is a bird because it has feathers.

And there are many kinds of birds...

There
are
birds
who

scratch
and grunt
and others
who soar
and hunt.

There are birds who are colorful and others who are bland.

There are birds that nest in trees, bushes, and, also in the sand.

But remember, a bird is a bird because it has feathers!

But what about the birds who have friends?

And those who go it alone? What about the birds kept in cages and the others who like to roam?

None of it matters, because at the end of the day, no matter what people say, A bird is a bird because it has feathers. And now YOU

know!

There are many other books by <u>Andi Cann</u>. Check them out at your favorite book seller!

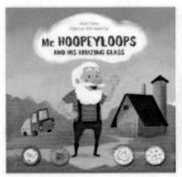  

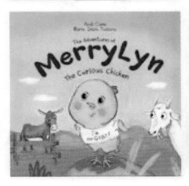  

We welcome you to include brief quotations in a review. If you would like to reproduce, store, or transmit the publication in whole or in part, please obtain written permission from the publisher. Otherwise, please do not store this publication in a retrieval system. Please do not transmit in any form or by any means electronic, mechanical, printing, photocopying, recording, or otherwise. Please honor our copyright! For permissions: Contact MindView Press via email: mindviewpress@gmail.com

Published by MindView Press: Hibou

ISBN-13:   978-1-949761-08-5   eBook

ISBN-13:   978-1-949761-13-9   Paperback

Thank you for reading!

Made in the USA
Columbia, SC
14 December 2018